Poetry for Young People
American Poetry

Edited by John Hollander

Sterling Publishing Co., Inc.
New York

For Adam, Lucy, and Noah
—*J.H.*
To my American Art teachers who perpetually inspire:
R. Bearden, T.H. Benton, R. Kent, A. Parker,
H. Pyle, B. Shahn, G.E. Wern
—*S.W.C.*

Library of Congress Cataloging-in-Publication Data

Poetry for young people : American poetry / edited by John
Hollander ; illustrated by Sally Wern Comport.

     p.   cm.

Includes index.

ISBN 1-4027-0517-4

   1. Children's poetry, American. 2. Young adult poetry,
American. [1. American poetry—Collections.] I. Hollander, John.
II. Comport, Sally Wern, ill.

PS586.3 .P643 2004

811.008'09282–dc22

                          2003024522

10   9   8   7   6   5   4   3   2   1

Published by Sterling Publishing Co., Inc.
387 Park Avenue South, New York, N.Y. 10016
Text ©2004 by John Hollander
Illustrations © 2004 by Sally Wern Comport
Distributed in Canada by Sterling Publishing
c/o Canadian Manda Group, One Atlantic Avenue, Suite 105
Toronto, Ontario, Canada M6K 3E7
Distributed in Great Britain and Europe by Chris Lloyd
463 Ashley Road, Parkstone, Poole, Dorset, BH14 0AX, England
Distributed in Australia by Capricorn Link (Australia) Pty Ltd.
P.O. Box 6651, Baulkham Hills, Business Centre, NSW 2153, Australia

Sterling ISBN 1–4027–0517–4

CONTENTS

INTRODUCTION

"I hear America singing, the varied carols I hear," writes the great poet Walt Whitman in the first of the poems in this book (pages 8–9). It serves well to introduce all those that follow, for it celebrates a variety of very particular voices, and then connects them all in the voice of America itself. Whitman takes great care to show that they do not blend together, but keep their distinctness while being harmonious. The old motto of the United States of America, *e pluribus unum* (out of many, one), referred originally to the federation of different states into one nation. But it has come to mean something very important about our culture, our civilization, which has been celebrated by many of our country's most interesting writers.

Our differences as individuals actually unite us in a unique way. The poems in this collection are by a variety of writers from the nineteenth and twentieth centuries, and they all concern the United States as a nation "conceived," as Lincoln put it in the Gettysburg Address "in liberty." But they speak of their concerns in a great variety of poetic voices, almost as if each poem and its way of talking were like an individual person, each different, all American. They were written by men and women with diverse concerns, backgrounds, and attitudes, and these poems, quite different from each other, are all, sometimes in very different ways, about the United States of America. Some of them directly address the nation as a subject or topic; many of them have to do with people or places or events that are significant in our country's history. But in either case, the ways of human life they respond to are American ones.

We know that no one of the fifty states, no matter how old or young as a member of the union, is more American than any other, just as no region of our part of the continent—north, south, east, west, middle and in-betweens—is the only American one. Deserts, forests, mountains, plains, valleys, seashores, none of these is more land-like than any other. And yet any one of them can, in a poem or a story or a painting, be made to seem, for the moment, like The Land itself. Farm, village, town, city; river, stream, lake, trail, footpath, road, highway; bridge and railroad—none is more essentially American than any other. But the American imagination itself has been able, on any new occasion, to make each of these seem to be the country's center.

Whitman spoke of America "singing," and we should remember that poems are like songs without music. But they compose their own musical accompaniments in the rhythmic beat and the grouping of speech sounds of their own words.

For one thing, poems can of course tell stories: they can do this clearly and amusingly, as in that famous ballad of baseball, "Casey at the Bat" (pages 30–33). It recounts what could be a tragedy—the fall of a hero—but in a comic manner.

Another kind of popular figure is seriously treated as a sort of hero in "Portrait VIII" by e.e.cummings (page 23), but in a half-comic way that avoids being solemn or stuffy. Poets have always known that being serious and being funny aren't always opposites—they frequently go together, the way being solemn and being silly sometimes do.

Stories can be told a little more indirectly or mysteriously, as in Edwin Arlington Robinson's "The House on the Hill" (page 34), about which we are told so little, or the brief account that the speaker of "Stopping by Woods on a Snowy Evening" (page 35) gives to himself about what is happening in the present moment.

Poems can even tell stories that are really about something else, something more general, like the parables in both the Old and New Testaments. Wallace Stevens' strange and puzzling "Anecdote of the Jar" (page 22), about how art can help organize nature, is one of these.

But poems can do a variety of other things as well. They can make up lists and catalogues, not to use for shopping but to recite, or think about. : Stephen Vincent Benét's "American Names" (pages 10–11) is one of these, as are "Indian Names" (pages 12–13) by Lydia Huntley Sigourney and, of course, Walt Whitman's "I Hear America Singing."

Poems can commemorate important events, most often far more intensely and certainly more briefly than speeches can. Such events include moments of our country in defense of itself at war: Francis Scott Key's verses on "The Defence of Fort McHenry" (page 18), which we all know under its later title, "The Star-Spangled Banner," speaks of a moment in battle, almost like a news report. Ralph Waldo Emerson's "Concord Hymn" (page 15) reminds us of a fight in the Revolutionary War. It was composed for the dedication of a monument—making a kind of monument of words. And this is also the case with Emma Lazarus's "The New Colossus" (page 20), composed for the dedication of the Statue of Liberty, although it celebrates one of America's great missions of peace, rather than war. And the publication of Oliver Wendell Holmes' "Old Ironsides" (page 16) resulted in a monument being created from a relic of past naval victories that would otherwise have been destroyed.

Poems can do something like sing songs. A popular poem about the death of Abraham Lincoln, "O Captain, My Captain" (page 24) is the only poem of Walt Whitman's that rhymes and seems song-like. And like songs, poems can vary widely in tone: they can be cheerful, like Henry Van

Dyke's "America for Me" (page 44), or even bitter, like Claude McKay's "America" (page 45). Emerson's "Concord Hymn" even suggests a protestant hymn in its meter and some of its phrasing, but it has nothing to do with any church or any organized religion whatsoever.

Some of these poems compare and contrast America with Europe, like the ones by Henry Van Dyke and William Cullen Bryant.

Some recall and think about American rivers. Hamlin Garland's "On the Mississippi" (page 41) gives us a wonderful glimpse of that great river at night. T.S. Eliot's "Virginia" (page 40) seems almost to be humming a tune to a remembered river. Langston Hughes' "The Negro Speaks of Rivers" (pages 26–27) treats rivers almost as ancient myths.

Two of the poems contemplate railroads, with strong attention and deep amusement, as in Emily Dickinson's "The Amherst Train" (page 38), and very differently in "The Engine" by Ella Wheeler Wilcox (page 39).

And some of the poems here are devoted to works of art. In May Swenson's wonderful descriptive poem, "A Navajo Blanket" (page 14), the poet celebrates a uniquely American kind of art. And William Cullen Bryant warns his friend, in "To an American Painter, Departing for Europe" (pages 28–29), to keep his American eye open as he views the wonders of the past that he has only read about or seen in pictures. Carl Sandburg in his "Jazz Fantasia" (page 43) feels the urgent power of America's own kind of music.

Taken together, all these poems give the reader a sense of the varieties of American experience across time and place. In some instances, they remind us of the different things imaginative minds notice in a particular event. Vachel Lindsay's poem about Fourth-of-July fireworks, "The Rockets That Reached Saturn" (page 46-47), presents us with a wondrous display that could never actually be seen. The first seven lines might almost be spoken by a child, the rest of it, by a poet. But part of the poem says ordinary things about shows of fireworks.

Ordinarily, we hear a siren or a screech, turn, look and notice a fire engine speeding by. But William Carlos Williams' "The Great Figure" (page 36–37), concerns one detail of the passing fire truck that perhaps only a child or a poet would think important. Noticing such things in various ways could be called "unofficial experiences," and we need poets and novelists and very good films to keep reminding us of them.

Poems differ most obviously from speeches or essays or stories by the forms of their verse. Some of the poems here are written in a form that English poetry has used since the early sixteenth century   the sonnet. The poems by Emma Lazarus, William Cullen Bryant, and Claude McKay, all fourteen lines long and in rhymed five-beat lines, are in sonnet form.

There are song-like poems in stanzas with *refrains*—lines at the end of stanzas that keep recurring—like "The Defence of Fort McHenry" and "America for Me." Refrains are also used very interestingly in "The House on the Hill."

Some of the poems in this book are in *free verse*—using lines that don't beat out rhythms of equal numbers of strong and weaker syllables, but move in rhythms of their own. Walt Whitman's free-verse lines always end where a sentence or clause or phrase stops, and his sentences never run over into the lines that follow (rhymed verse will often do this). But the free verse of twentieth-century poets developed many interesting forms. William Carlos Williams, T.S. Eliot, May Swenson, e.e. cummings, Carl Sandburg, and Langston Hughes, in the poems printed here, show this clearly. Their different ways of shaping lines to grammatical units, of composing stanzas, of making rhythm more or less audible, all remind us of the importance of form for all poetry.

As we read through these poems, in all their variety, we may be reminded of Walt Whitman's remark that "the United States, themselves, are essentially the greatest poem." But only one of America's very greatest poets could make that statement.

I HEAR AMERICA SINGING
Walt Whitman (1819–1892)

Many of the "varied carols" of so many different Americans are sung at work, and many are sung before or after work, too. Without saying so, Walt Whitman blends them into a grand chorus that illustrates the motto of the United States of America (up to 1956): "e pluribus unum"—out of many, one. For this very great poet, it is appropriate to a celebration of America for each to sing his or her own song rather than for everyone to sing the same song together.

I hear America singing, the varied carols I hear,
Those of mechanics, each one singing his as it should be blithe
      and strong,
The carpenter singing his as he measures his plank or beam,
The mason singing his as he makes ready for work, or leaves off
      work,
The boatman singing what belongs to him in his boat, the
      deckhand singing on the steamboat deck,
The shoemaker singing as he sits on his bench, the hatter
      singing as he stands,
The wood-cutter's song, the ploughboy's on his way in the
      morning, or at noon intermission or at sundown,
The delicious singing of the mother, or of the young wife at
      work, or of the girl sewing or washing,
Each singing what belongs to him or her and to none else,
The day what belongs to the day—at night the party of young
      fellows, robust, friendly,
Singing with open mouths their strong melodious songs.

blithe—*happy, carefree*
hatter—*hat maker*
robust—*healthy, strong*
melodious—*musical*

FROM "AMERICAN NAMES"
Stephen Vincent Benét (1898–1943)

Some knowledge and love of foreign places and customs can make us value familiar ones more highly. This is often because we get to notice aspects of those familiar things that we had not paid attention to before. The speaker of this poem has obviously been abroad in Europe and read a great deal about it, and names of places there mean a good deal to him. But he is most fascinated by the improvised, often funny, sound of those of his native country.

I have fallen in love with American names,
The sharp names that never get fat,
The snakeskin-titles of mining-claims,
The plumed war-bonnet of Medicine Hat,
Tucson and Deadwood and Lost Mule Flat.

Seine and Piave are silver spoons,
But the spoonbowl-metal is thin and worn,
There are English counties like hunting-tunes
Played on the keys of a postboy's horn,
But I will remember where I was born.

I will remember Carquinez Straits,
Little French Lick and Lundy's Lane,
The Yankee ships and the Yankee dates
And the bullet-towns of Calamity Jane.
I will remember Skunktown Plain.

***

I shall not rest quiet in Montparnasse.
I shall not lie easy at Winchelsea.
You may bury my body in Sussex grass,
You may bury my tongue at Champmedy.
I shall not be there. I shall rise and pass.
Bury my heart at Wounded Knee.

Medicine Hat—*town, actually not in the U.S. but in Alberta, Canada*
Tucson—*city in Arizona*
Deadwood—*there are towns in California, Idaho, New Mexico, Oregon, Texas and South Dakota called "Deadwood"*
Lost Mule Flat—*probably Lost Mule Canyon in northwest Texas*
Seine—*(pronounced "sen")—river running through Paris*
Piave—*(pronounced "pYAHvay")—river in northern Italy*
postboy—*mail carrier*
Carquinez Straits—*this is a channel in a bay in Solano County, California*
Little French Lick—*"French Lick" is a town in Indiana*
Lundy's Lane—*near Niagara Falls and site of an important battle in the War of 1812*
Bullet towns of Calamity Jane—*Martha Jane Burk (1852–1903), frontierswoman known as "Calamity Jane" was famous for her shooting and riding; she lived in the violent towns of Virginia City, Montana and, later, Deadwood, South Dakota*
Skunktown Plain—*"Skunktown" is a town in Nevada*
Montparnasse—*(pronounced "mawpahrnahss") district in Paris*
Winchelsea—*town in Sussex, in southern England*
Sussex—*county in the south of England*
Champmedy—*(pronounced "chahmaydee") scene of battle in France in World War I*
Wounded Knee—*Creek in South Dakota where U.S. troops massacred many Sioux in 1890*

INDIAN NAMES
Lydia Huntley Sigourney (1791–1865)

The oldest American place-names—those of lakes, rivers, and mountains—come from Native American languages. It is as if ghosts of the Native Americans who were killed and displaced, first by European settlers, then by their descendants, will always haunt us. Mrs. Sigourney was a popular sentimental poet who lived and worked in Hartford, Connecticut, in the first part of the nineteenth century; she also wrote an epic poem about Native American life.

"How can the red men be forgotten, while so many
of our states and territories, bays, lakes, and rivers,
are indelibly stamped by names of their giving?"

Ye say they all have passed away,
  That noble race and brave,
That their light canoes have vanished
  From off the crested wave;
That 'mid the forests where they roamed
  There rings no hunter's shout,
But their name is on your waters,
  Ye may not wash it out.

'Tis where Ontario's billow
  Like Ocean's surge is curled,
Where strong Niagara's thunders wake
  The echo of the world.
Where red Missouri bringeth
  Rich tribute from the west,
And Rappahannock sweetly sleeps
  On green Virginia's breast.

Ye say their cone-like cabins,
  That clustered o'er the vale,
Have fled away like withered leaves,
  Before the autumn gale,
But their memory liveth on your hills,
  Their baptism on your shore,
Your everlasting rivers speak
  Their dialect of yore.

Old Massachusetts wears it,
  Within her lordly crown,
And broad Ohio bears it,
  Amid his young renown;
Connecticut hath wreathed it
  Where her quiet foliage waves,
And bold Kentucky breathed it hoarse
  Through all her ancient caves.

Wachuset hides its lingering voice
  Within his rocky heart,
And Alleghany graves its tone
  Throughout his lofty chart;
Monadnock on his forehead hoar
  Doth seal the sacred trust,
Your mountains build their monument,
  Though ye destroy their dust.

Ye call these red-browed brethren
  The insects of an hour,
Crushed like the noteless worm amid
  The regions of their power;
Ye drive them from their fathers' lands,
  Ye break of faith the seal,
But can ye from the court of Heaven
  Exclude their last appeal?

Ye see their unresisting tribes,
    With toilsome step and slow,
On through the trackless desert pass,
    A caravan of woe;
Think ye the Eternal's ear is deaf?
    His sleepless vision dim?
Think ye the soul's blood may not cry
    From that far land to him?

Rappahannock—*river in Virginia*

Wachuset—*mountain in Massachusetts: its name in Algonquian means "mountain-at"*

Monadnock—*mountain in New Hampshire: in Algonquian, "island-mountain,"*
    because it looked like an island rising from the water around it

hoar—*white with age*

13

A NAVAJO BLANKET
May Swenson (1919–1989)

May Swenson, one of the finest and most original poets of her time, came from Utah, but wrote her poems in and near New York. She was always interested in visual patterns, in what she saw and in arrangements of poems on the page. Here she leads the reader's eye on a journey into, and then out of, a sort of maze of color and form. The thread of green "secretly crosses the border" in two senses: it moves across the border of the blanket, and, in a playful way, it is like a spy or some other illegal immigrant slipping over a national boundary.

Eye-dazzlers the Indians wave. Three colors
are paths that pull you in, and pin you
to the maze. Brightness makes your eyes jump,
surveying the geometric field. Alight, and enter
any of the gates—of Blue. Of Red, or Black.
Be calmed and hooded, a hawk brought down,
glad to fasten to the forearm of a Chief.

You can sleep at the center,
attended by the sun that never fades, by Moon
that cools. Then, slipping free of zig-zag and
hypnotic diamond, find your way out
by the spirit trail, a faint Green thread that
secretly crosses the border, where your mind
is rinsed and returned to you like a white cup.

CONCORD HYMN
Ralph Waldo Emerson (1803–1882)

On April 19, 1775 Massachusetts militia men fought British regular troops at Concord, 20 miles northwest of Boston. This was the first battle of the Revolutionary War. Emerson's hymn was written for and sung at the completion of a monument at Concord, and is dated April 19, 1836. "The shot heard round the world" points out how influential the American Revolution was, particularly in France shortly before her own different kind of revolution. Emerson was most famous as a philosophical essayist, but his poetry is among the strongest in nineteenth century America.

By the rude bridge that arched the flood
   Their flag to April's breeze unfurled.
Here once the embattled farmers stood
   And fired the shot heard round the world.

The foe long since in silence slept;
   Alike the conqueror silent sleeps;
And Time the ruined bridge has swept
   Down the dark stream which seaward creeps.

On this green bank, by this soft stream,
   We set today a votive stone;
That memory may their deed redeem,
   When, like our sires, our sons are gone.

Spirit, that made these heroes dare
   To die, and leave their children free,
Bid Time and Nature gently spare
   The shaft we raise to them and thee.

flood—*fully flowing stream (here, the Concord River)*
votive—*dedicated*
sires—*forefathers*
shaft—*column*

15

OLD IRONSIDES
Oliver Wendell Holmes (1809-1894)

An important medical researcher and professor of medicine at Harvard Medical School, Holmes wrote verse and novels as well as a great many literary essays. He wrote this poem in 1830 as a protest against the Navy Department's plan to scrap the Constitution, a frigate (sailing wooden warship) of 44 guns that had fought famously in the War of 1812. The frigate was named "Old Ironsides" because of her very strong and durable construction. The poem became very popular, and was effective in preserving the ship, which can still be visited in Boston.

Ay, tear her tattered ensign down!
   Long has it waved on high,
And many an eye has danced to see
   That banner in the sky;
Beneath it rung the battle shout,
   And burst the cannon's roar;—
The meteor of the ocean air
   Shall sweep the clouds no more.

Her deck, once red with heroes' blood,
   Where knelt the vanquished foe,
When winds were hurrying o'er the flood,
   And waves were white below,
No more shall feel the victor's tread,
   Or know the conquered knee;—
The harpies of the shore shall pluck
   The eagle of the sea!

Oh, better that her shattered hulk
   Should sink beneath the wave;
Her thunders shook the mighty deep,
   And there should be her grave;
Nail to the mast her holy flag,
   Set every threadbare sail,
And give her to the god of storms,
   The lightning and the gale!

ensign—*flag*
harpies—*unpleasant mythical monsters, half-bird, half-woman*

DEFENCE OF FORT MCHENRY
Francis Scott Key (1779-1843)

While on a negotiating mission during the War of 1812, a lawyer named Francis Scott Key was detained on board a British ship. From there he watched the bombardment of Fort McHenry, near Baltimore. His poem—its rhythms came from an English drinking-song—expressed his great joy and relief at the sight of the flag still waving the next morning. The song officially became the U.S. national anthem in 1931, but we seldom hear more than the first stanza. It is in the second one (perhaps the best) that gives us a sense of the feelings of the observer.

> *O! say can you see, by the dawn's early light,*
> *What so proudly we hail'd at the twilight's last gleaming,*
> *Whose broad stripes and bright stars through the perilous fight,*
> *O'er the ramparts we watch'd, were so gallantly streaming?*
> *And the rockets' red glare, the bombs bursting in air,*
> *Gave proof through the night that our flag was still there—*
> *O! say, does that star-spangled banner yet wave*
> *O'er the land of the free, and the home of the brave?*

On the shore, dimly seen through the mists of the deep,
Where the foe's haughty host in dread silence reposes,
What is that which the breeze o'er the towering steep,
As it fitfully blows, half conceals, half discloses?
Now it catches the gleam of the morning's first beam,
In full glory reflected now shines on the stream—
'Tis the star-spangled banner, O! long may it wave
O'er the land of the free, and the home of the brave.

And where is that band who so vauntingly swore
That the havock of war and the battle's confusion
A home and a country should leave us no more?
Their blood has wash'd out their foul foot-steps' pollution,
No refuge could save the hireling and slave,
From the terror of flight or the gloom of the grave;
And the star-spangled banner in triumph doth wave
O'er the land of the free, and the home of the brave.

O! thus be it ever when freemen shall stand
  Between their lov'd home, and the war's desolation,
Blest with vict'ry and peace, may the heav'n-rescued land
  Praise the power that hath made and preserv'd us a nation!
    Then conquer we must, when our cause it is just,
    And this be our motto—"In God is our trust!"
      And the star-spangled banner in triumph shall wave
      O'er the land of the free, and the home of the brave.

band—*in this case, the English*
vauntingly—*boastfully*
havock—*destruction*

19

THE NEW COLOSSUS
Emma Lazarus (1849-1887)

The "brazen giant of Greek fame" was the Colossus of Rhodes, a huge figure of the sun-god Helios commemorating a victory in battle. It stood at the entrance to the harbor of the city of Rhodes in ancient Greek and Roman times. The "new Colossus" is the Statue of Liberty, for which Emma Lazarus wrote this poem (it was recited at the dedication of the statue in 1866). A woman, a welcoming figure to all the immigrants coming to this country, represents the New World for Lazarus better than a menacing male god. She asks Europe not for its wealth and traditions but, rather surprisingly, for "your tired, your poor." New York's "air-bridged harbor" had at that time no actual bridges, and the "two cities" were New York and Brooklyn, which then were separate.

Not like the brazen giant of Greek fame,
With conquering limbs astride from land to land;
Here at our sea-washed, sunset gates shall stand
A mighty woman with a torch, whose flame
Is the imprisoned lightning, and her name
Mother of Exiles. From her beacon-hand
Glows world-wide welcome; her mild eyes command
The air-bridged harbor that twin cities frame.
"Keep, ancient lands, your storied pomp!" cries she
With silent lips. "Give me your tired, your poor,
Your huddled masses yearning to breathe free,
The wretched refuse of your teeming shore.
Send these, the homeless, tempest-tost to me,
I lift my lamp beside the golden door!"

brazen—*crude and shameless*—*(here, also made of brass)*
storied pomp—*famous splendor*
refuse—*waste (here, people rejected in any way by their native land)*

ANECDOTE OF THE JAR
Wallace Stevens (1879–1955)

Wallace Stevens, a greatly original and imaginative poet, lived in Hartford, Connecticut. In this strange and puzzling little "anecdote" (usually a very short story told aloud, often humorous, often about some famous person or event), the speaker tells of placing a jar not, as we might expect, "on a hill in Tennessee" but "in Tennessee" directly, as if the small jar were important enough to create order in the wild landscape of a whole state. The jar seen from above looks round, and that word echoes through the first two stanzas in surround, around, and finally, ground. The jar is not decorative, but it is so unlike nature, so much a product of human art, that it can rule everywhere from its hill, like a king from his throne. Unlike so many stories of the pushing back of wilderness along the American frontier going westward, this anecdote tells of a mental, rather than physical, event.

I placed a jar in Tennessee,
And round it was, upon a hill.
It made the slovenly wilderness
Surround that hill.

The wilderness rose up to it
And sprawled around, no longer wild.
The jar was round upon the ground
And tall and of a port in air.

It took dominion everywhere.
The jar was gray and bare.
It did not give of bird nor bush
Like nothing else in Tennessee.

slovenly—*carelessly messy or sloppy*
of a port—*having a certain bearing or posture and also having a certain import or meaning*
took dominion-*controlled, ruled over*

PORTRAIT VIII
e.e. cummings (1894–1962)

*Buffalo Bill (William F. Cody, 1846–1917) was a famous
figure who for decades represented the "wild west," having been a
cavalry scout and buffalo hunter. Eventually, he ran "Buffalo
Bill's Wild West Show," which toured the U.S. and Europe. The
word "defunct" is used in two senses here: "dead," and also
"extinct, obsolete." cummings (he always spelled his name in
lower-case) did a lot of typographical experiments in his poems.
In this one, for instance, he runs the numbers of the clay pigeons
together to express how rapid the shooting was. This poem may
also be about the death of the Old West itself.*

Buffalo Bill's
defunct
     who used to
     ride a watersmooth-silver
               stallion
and break onetwothreefourfive pigeonsjustlikethat
                          Jesus

he was a handsome man
            and what i want to know is
how do you like your blueeyed boy
Mister Death

pigeons—*clay pigeons, ceramic disks for target practice*

O CAPTAIN! MY CAPTAIN!
Walt Whitman (1819–1892)

This famous poem about the death of Abraham Lincoln has a kind of sing-song meter and rhyme, which Whitman never used in the rest of his poetry. The metaphor of a ship for a national state is a very old one. Well before the Civil War, Henry Wadsworth Longfellow had urged the Union to "Sail on, O Ship of State!" In Whitman's poem, Lincoln is the captain who dies bringing the ship safely to port.

O Captain! my Captain! our fearful trip is
    done;
The ship has weather'd every rack, the prize
    we sought is won;
The port is near, the bells I hear, the people
    all exulting,
While follow eyes the steady keel, the vessel
    grim and daring;
  But O heart! heart! heart!
    O the bleeding drops of red,
      Where on the deck my Captain lies,
      Fallen cold and dead.

O Captain! my Captain! rise up and hear the
      bells;
Rise up—for you the flag is flung—for you the
      bugle trills;
For you bouquets and ribbon'd wreaths—for
      you the shores a-crowding;
For you they call, the swaying mass, their eager
      faces turning;
  Here, Captain! dear father!
    This arm beneath your head;
      It is some dream that on the deck,
        You've fallen cold and dead.

My Captain does not answer, his lips are pale
      and still,
My father does not feel my arm, he has no pulse
      nor will,
The ship is anchor'd safe and sound, its voyage
      closed and done,
From fearful trip the victor ship comes in with
      object won;
  Exult O shores, and ring O bells!
    But I, with mournful tread,
      Walk the deck my Captain lies,
        Fallen cold and dead.

rack—*violence of a storm*

THE NEGRO SPEAKS OF RIVERS
Langston Hughes (1902-1967)

Rivers are traditional and continuing symbols of time, of change and stability at once, and of historical times and places. Here, in addition, the poet's own voice (his poetic soul) seems itself to be a master-river flowing through the times and places in the poem. Hughes was a very important African-American poet of the twentieth century, and this poem speaks both to his own condition and to that of all Americans of imagination. It suggests that we should all "know rivers," both near and far in time and place, the better to know ourselves.

I've known rivers:
I've known rivers ancient as the world and older than
      the flow of human blood in human veins.

My soul has grown deep like the rivers.

I bathed in the Euphrates when dawns were young.
I built my hut near the Congo and it lulled me to sleep.
I looked upon the Nile and raised the pyramids above it.
I heard the singing of the Mississippi when Abe Lincoln went down to
      New Orleans, and I've seen its muddy bosom turn all golden
      in the sunset.

I've known rivers:
Ancient, dusky rivers.

My soul has grown deep like the rivers.

Euphrates—*river in Mesopotamia (spoken of in Hughes' day as "the cradle of
   civilization")*

TO AN AMERICAN PAINTER DEPARTING FOR EUROPE
William Cullen Bryant (1794–1878)

Thomas Cole was a major painter of splendid landscapes who in 1829 went to Europe for the first time. His friend, the poet William Cullen Bryant, thought of him wandering through so many European historical places and scenes. He wrote this sonnet to encourage Cole to retain his unique American vision of nature which he calls, in the last line, "that wilder image." The splendid language of the poem makes us hear effects like those in paintings, such as the "eyes," "light" and rhyming "skies" they see in the first line. And if you read lines 4 through 8 aloud, the landscape, with its "wilder image" comes tos life.

Thine eyes shall see the light of distant skies:
    Yet, Cole! Thy heart shall bear to Europe's strand
    A living image of our own bright land,
Such as upon thy glorious canvass lies.
Lone lakes—savannahs where the bison roves—
    Rocks rich with summer garlands—solemn streams—
    Skies, where the desert eagle wheels and screams—
Spring bloom and autumn blaze of boundless groves.
Fair scenes shall greet thee where thou goest—fair,
    But different—everywhere the trace of men,
    Paths, homes, graves, ruins, from the lowest glen
To where life shrinks from the fierce Alpine air.
    Gaze on them, till the tears shall dim thy sight,
    But keep that earlier, wilder image bright.

Thine—*older, familiar form of "yours", as with "thou" equals "you" and "thee" equals "to you"*
strand—*shore*
savannahs—*treeless, flat grasslands*
bison—*American buffalo*
fair—*means "beautiful" here*

CASEY AT THE BAT
Ernest Thayer (1863-1940)

This celebrated poem is still quoted and imitated by newspaper sports writers after well over a hundred years. It was written in 188
by a humor columnist for a San Francisco newspaper, but the events in its amusingly told story continue to occur. Somewhere, all ov
the country, some arrogant Casey will always be striking out.

The outlook wasn't brilliant for the Mudville
    nine that day;
The score stood four to two with but one
    inning more to play.
And then when Cooney died at first, and
    Barrows did the same,
A sickly silence fell upon the patrons of the
    game.

A straggling few got up to go in deep despair.
    The rest
Clung to that hope which springs eternal in the
    human breast;
They thought if only Casey could but get a
    whack at that—
We'd put up even money now with Casey at
    the bat.

But Flynn preceded Casey, as did also Jimmy
    Blake.
And the former was a lulu, and the latter was a
    cake;
So upon that stricken multitude grim melancholy
    sat.
For there seemed but little chance of Casey's
    getting to the bat.

But Flynn let drive a single, to the wonderment of all,
And Blake, the much despised, tore the cover off the ball;
And when the dust had lifted, and men saw what had
            occurred,
There was Johnnie safe at second and Flynn a-hugging third.

Then from 5,000 throats and more there rose a lusty yell;
It rumbled through the valley, it rattled in the dell;
It pounded on the mountain and recoiled upon the flat,
For Casey, mighty Casey, was advancing to the bat.

There was ease in Casey's manner as he stepped into his place;
There was pride in Casey's bearing and a smile lit Casey's
            face.
And when, responding to the cheers, he lightly doffed his hat,
No stranger in the crowd could doubt 'twas Casey at the bat.

Ten thousand eyes were on him as he rubbed his hands with
            dirt;
Five thousand tongues applauded when he wiped them on
            his shirt;
Then while the writhing pitcher ground the ball into his hip,
Defiance gleamed in Casey's eye, a sneer curled Casey's lip.

And now the leather-covered sphere came hurtling through
            the air,
And Casey stood a-watching it in haughty grandeur
            there.
Close by the sturdy batsman the ball unheeded sped—
"That ain't my style," said Casey. "Strike one," the umpire said.

From the benches, black with people, there went up a
            muffled roar,
Like the beating of the storm-waves on a worn and distant
            shore.
"Kill him! Kill the umpire!" shouted someone on the stand,
And it's likely they'd have killed him had not Casey raised his
            shand.

31

With a smile of Christian charity great Casey's visage shone;
He stilled the rising tumult; he bade the game go on;
He signaled to the pitcher and once more the spheroid flew;
But Casey still ignored it and the umpire said, "Strike two."

"Fraud!" cried the maddened thousands, and the echo answered "Fraud!"
But one scornful look from Casey and the audience was awed.
They saw his face grow stern and cold, they saw his muscles strain,
And they knew that Casey wouldn't let that ball go by again.

The sneer is gone from Casey's lip, his teeth are clinched in hate,
He pounds with cruel violence his bat upon the plate;
And now the pitcher holds the ball, and now he lets it go,
And now the air is shattered by the force of Casey's blow.

Oh, somewhere in this favoured land the sun is shining bright,
The band is playing somewhere, and somewhere hearts are light;
And somewhere men are laughing, and somewhere children shout,
But there is no joy in Mudville—mighty Casey has struck out.

lulu, cake—*weak hitters (sarcastic)*   writhing—*twisting*
stricken—*struck (with despair)*   batsman—*batter*
lusty—*energetic*   visage—*face*
dell—*small valley*   tumult—*noise*
doffed—*tipped*   spheroid—*the ball*

THE HOUSE ON THE HILL
Edwin Arlington Robinson (1869-1935)

Robinson was born and grew up in Maine, and much of his earlier poetry is set in an imaginary town in that state. In a New England town, the house of the richest would often be on a hill, and the house in this poem is one of those. This kind of poem, called a villanelle, alternates two refrains (lines that repeat throughout the poem). Notice how the second one keeps changing its meaning slightly ("nothing more to say," to say about what?) until at the very end, the poem itself seems to have learned that it is time to stop.

They are all gone away;
　The House is shut and still,
There is nothing more to say.

Through broken walls and gray
　The winds blow bleak and shrill
They are all gone away.

Nor is there one to-day
　To speak them good or ill:
There is nothing more to say.

Why is it then we stay
　Around that sunken sill?
They are all gone away,

And our poor fancy-play
　For them is wasted skill:
There is nothing more to say.

There is rain and decay
　In the House on the Hill:
They have all gone away,
There is nothing more to say.

sill—*door- or windowsill*
fancy-play—*an imagined story*

34

STOPPING BY WOODS ON A SNOWY EVENING
Robert Frost (1874–1963)

Robert Frost was born in San Francisco, but is always thought of as the great twentieth century poet of New England. The speaker's midwinter journey may be toward the village or from it; his errand may be business or love or friendship (the "promises to keep"). In this poem he pauses, despite the cold and the piling snow, to look at the woods that are "lovely" because they are "dark and deep." And even though the woods are private property, he knows he is not disturbing the owner's personal privacy ("His house is in the village") at the time. The last line is repeated almost sleepily, but perhaps also because it means something slightly different the second time, about some other kind of journey.

Whose woods these are I think I know.
His house is in the village though;
He will not mind me stopping here
To see his woods fill up with snow.

My little horse must think it queer
To stop without a farmhouse near
Between the woods and frozen lake
The darkest evening of the year.

He gives his harness-bells a shake
To ask if there is some mistake.
The only other sound's the sweep
Of easy wind and downy flake.

The woods are lovely, dark and deep,
But I have promises to keep,
And miles to go before I sleep,
And miles to go before I sleep.

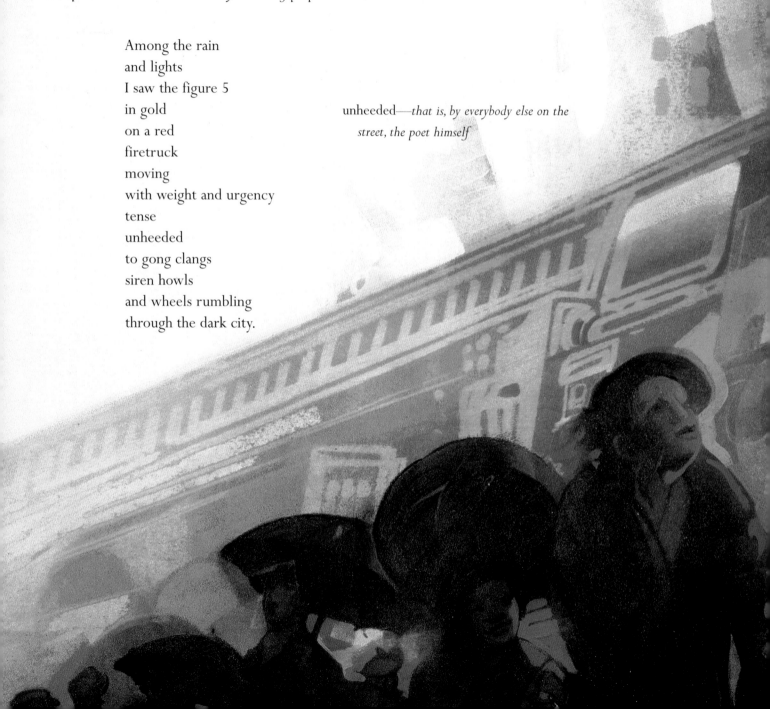

THE GREAT FIGURE
William Carlos Williams (1883–1963)

Williams, one of the twentieth century's finest poets, was also a doctor and lived in Rutherford, New Jersey. Visiting a friend in New York City one day, he heard the "clatter of bells" and the roar of a fire engine going by at the end of the street. He later wrote: "I turned just in time to see a golden figure 5 on a red background flash by." The impression it made was so strong that he called the poem he wrote about "The Great Figure." This celebrated the quickly passing beauty of the glimpse of the numeral 5 on the fire truck; but it also made fun of so-called "great figures" in public life who seemed less important than those "heeded" by crowds of people.

Among the rain
and lights
I saw the figure 5
in gold
on a red
firetruck
moving
with weight and urgency
tense
unheeded
to gong clangs
siren howls
and wheels rumbling
through the dark city.

unheeded—that is, by everybody else on the street, the poet himself

THE AMHERST TRAIN
Emily Dickinson (1830–1886)

Emily Dickinson, one of our greatest poets, lived in Amherst, Massachusetts. Her very personal imagination focussed on observations of small, ordinary events and made them seem most unusual. Here, she sees a local train, from a distance, as a kind of horse, part wild, part domestic. Her calling the bursts of the train-whistle "stanzas" reminds us that the single long sentence making up her poem runs through its lines and stanzas like a kind of train of thought.

I like to see it lap the miles,
And lick the valleys up,
And stop to feed itself at tanks;
And then, prodigious, step

Around a pile of mountains,
And, supercilious, peer
In shanties by the sides of roads;
And then a quarry pare

To fit its sides, and crawl between,
Complaining all the while
In horrid, hooting stanza;
Then chase itself down hill

And neigh like Boanerges;
Then, punctual as a star,
Stop—docile and omnipotent—
At is own stable door.

prodigious—*huge*
supercilious—*disdainfully proud*
quarry—*pit from which stone is cut*
pare—*slide by so closely as to be almost peeling the surface*
   of the rock in the quarry
Boanerges—*In the New Testament (Mark III), James and*
   John, sons of Zebedee, were called by this name meaning
   "sons of thunder."
docile—*gentle*
omnipotent—*all powerful*

THE ENGINE
Ella Wheeler Wilcox (1850–1919)

*This is a very different view of a steam locomotive from the one
that pulled the train in Emily Dickinson's poem. For Mrs. Wilcox,
there is no amusing distance between the speaker and the engine's
immense power, speed, and potential for violence were it to go off
the track that it hates for constraining it. The rhythm of her language expresses its burning energy and forward motion.*

Into the gloom of the deep, dark night,
    With panting breath and a startled scream;
Swift as a bird in sudden flight,
    Darts this creature of steel and steam.

Awful dangers are lurking nigh,
    Rocks and chasms are near the track,
But straight by the light of its great white eye,
    It speeds through the shadows, dense and black.

Terrible thoughts and fierce desires
    Trouble its mad heart many an hour,
Where burn and smoulder the hidden fires,
    Coupled ever with might and power.

It hates, as a wild horse hates the rein,
    The narrow track by vale and hill:
And shrieks with a cry of startled pain;
    And longs to follow its own wild will.

nigh—*near*
chasms—*deep clefts in the earth*
smoulder—*burn slowly without flame*
vale—*valley*

VIRGINIA
T.S. Eliot (1888-1965)

This poem is one of a group called "Landscapes" by this great American-born poet who lived and worked in England, but who is remembering a scene from his earlier home. The river here is slow and almost autumnal, and seems itself to be speaking the last four lines. Its "iron thoughts" may be those of the iron ore in its bed that reddens the stream.

Red river, red river,
Slow flow heat is silence
No will is still as a river
Still. Will heat move
Only through the mocking-bird
Heard once? Still hills
Wait. Gates wait. Purple trees,
White trees, wait, wait,
Delay, decay. Living, living,
Never moving. Ever moving
Iron thoughts came with me
And go with me:
Red river, river river.

40

ON THE MISSISSIPPI
Hamlin Garland (1860–1940)

This little sketch is from a book of poems called Prairie
Songs *by Hamlin Garland, best known as a writer of
stories and novels of midwestern rural life. Recording a
moment on the great river, it celebrates without cheering
or raising its voice, but by devotedly observing and
quietly describing.*

Through wild and tangled forests
The broad, unhasting river flows—
Spotted with rain-drops, gray with night;
    Upon its curving breast there goes
A lonely steamboat's larboard light,
    A blood-red star against the shadowy oaks;
Noiseless as a ghost, through greenish gleam
Of fire-flies, before the boat's wild scream—
    A heron flaps away
    Like silence taking flight.

unhasting—*unhurrying*
larboard—*port, or left, side of a boat*
heron—*long-necked wading bird*

41

HARLEM HOPSCOTCH
Maya Angelou (1928—)

Maya Angelou is a very popular writer. In this little children's rhyme, the poet is speaking in the voice of a little African-American girl playing hopscotch on the sidewalk of a street in Harlem, in New York City. She weaves together thoughts of her game and of the hard realities of the life around her. At then end, we may wonder what "lost" and "won" may refer to—the hopscotch game (probably fair)? The struggle to grow up successfully in an unfair world? Or perhaps both.

One foot down, then hop! It's hot.
    Good things for the ones that's got.
Another jump, now to the left.
      Everybody for hisself.

In the air, now both feet down.
    Since you black, don't stick around.
Food is gone, the rent is due,
      Curse and cry and then jump two.

All the people out of work,
    Hold for three, then twist and jerk.
Cross the line, they count you out.
        That's what hopping's all about.

Both feet flat, the game is done.
They think I lost. I think I won.

Jazz Fantasia
Carl Sandburg (1878–1967)

Carl Sandburg came from Illinois and wrote about Chicago. In the early 1920's, that city was becoming a center for jazz, and Sandburg would have heard great musicians like King Oliver and Louis Armstrong playing in person. This poem celebrates jazz for its energy and some of its sadness, and at the end, the poet reminds us of how jazz started in New Orleans and came up the Mississippi to Chicago and Kansas City.

Drum on your drums, batter on your banjos,
sob on the long cool winding saxophones.
Go to it, jazzmen.

Sling your knuckles on the bottoms of the happy
tin pans, let your trombones ooze, and go husha-
husha-hush with the slippery sand-paper.

Moan like an autumn wind high in the lonesome tree-
tops, moan soft like you wanted something terrible,
cry like a racing car slipping away from a motorcycle
cop, bang-bang! you jazzmen, bang altogether drums,
traps, banjoes, horns, tin cans—make two people fight
on the top of a stairway and scratch each other's eyes
in a clinch tumbling down the stairs.

Can the rough stuff. . . now a Mississippi steamboat
pushes up the night river with a hoo-hoo-hoo—oo. . .
and the green lanterns calling to the high soft stars
. . . and a red moon rides on the humps of the low river
hills . . . go to it, O jazzmen.

AMERICA FOR ME
Henry Van Dyke (1852–1933)

Van Dyke was a Presbyterian minister, a Princeton professor, and for a while a diplomat in the Netherlands who wrote novels, many essays, and some verses. The sentiments in this poem are those of an educated and well-traveled man before World War I. They depend on rather simpler attitudes than most of us hold today, but despite this, we can all feel something of this poem's sense of our nation as a homeland.

'Tis fine to see the Old World, and travel up and down
Among the famous palaces and cities of renown,
To admire the crumbly castles and the statues of the kings,—
But now I think I've had enough of antiquated things.

So it's home again, and home again, America for me!
My heart is turning home again, and there I long to be,
In the land of youth and freedom beyond the ocean bars,
Where the air is full of sunlight and the flag is full of stars!

Oh, London is a man's town, there's power in the air;
And Paris is a woman's town, with flowers in her hair;
And it's sweet to dream in Venice, and it's great to study Rome;
But when it comes to living there is no place like home.

I like the German fir-woods, in green battalions drilled;
I like the gardens of Versailles with flashing fountains filled;
But, oh, to take your hand, my dear, and ramble for a day
In the friendly western woodland where Nature has her way!

I know that Europe's wonderful, yet something seems to lack:
The Past is too much with her, and the people looking back.
But the glory of the Present is to make the Future free,—
We love our land for what she is and what she is to be.

Oh, it's home again, and home again, America for me!
I want a ship that's westward bound to plough the rolling sea,
To the bléssed Land of Room Enough beyond the ocean bars,
Where the air is full of sunlight and the flag is full of stars.

Versailles—*site of the grand palace of King Louis XIV of France*

44

AMERICA
Claude McKay (1889–1948)

Claude McKay, poet and novelist, was born in Jamaica but came to the United States in 1912, when in his early twenties. This African-American of the earlier twentieth century views his adopted country as "a cultured hell." But he speaks of drawing on its energy, and gaining some of its "bigness." His dark vision of the future sees monuments and skyscrapers, "granite wonders," giving way, like older civilizations, to Timess itself.

Although she feeds me bread of bitterness,
And sinks into my throat her tiger's tooth,
Stealing my breath of life, I will confess
I love this cultured hell that tests my youth!
Her vigor flows like tides into my blood,
Giving me strength erect against her hate.
Her bigness sweeps my being like a flood.
Yet as a rebel fronts a king in state,
I stand within her walls with not a shred
Of terror, malice, not a word of jeer.
Darkly I gaze into the days ahead,
And see her might and granite wonders there,
Beneath the touch of Time's unerring hand,
Like priceless treasures sinking in the sand.

fronts—*confronts*
in state—*in public view*

45

THE ROCKETS THAT REACHED SATURN

chel Lindsay (1879–1931)

imaginative look at Fourth-of-July
rks, the poet discovers that the beauty of the
rks and the importance of our great national holiday are
y significant: each of them outlasts the celebration. This
ees the rockets as having their own Independence Day as
olors and lights end up in a different world.

On the Fourth of July sky rockets went up
Over the church and the trees and the town,
Stripes and stars, riding red cars.
Each rocket wore a red-white-and-blue gown,
And I did not see one rocket come down.

Next day on the hill I found dead sticks,
Scorched like blown-out candle-wicks.

But where are the rockets? Up in the sky.
As for the sticks, let them lie.
Dead sticks are not the Fourth of July.

n Saturn they grow like wonderful weeds,
n some ways like weeds of ours,
Twisted and beautiful, straight and awry,
But nodding all day to the heavenly powers.
The stalks are smoke,
And the blossoms green light,
And crystalline fireworks flowers.

awry—twisted
crystalline—crystal-like, glistening

46

INDEX